PASSING CLOUDS

Jonathan Bennett

PASSING CLOUDS

First published 2008

Published by Jonathan Bennett
Pippins, Ramsdean Road, Petersfield, GU32 3PJ

Cover: *Heath Pond, Petersfield*
Photographed by John Wigley CPAGB

Typeset by John Owen Smith, Headley Down

© Jonathan Bennett

All rights reserved. No part of this book may be reprinted, reproduced, utilised in any form mechanical, or other means known or hereafter in any form invented including photocopying and recording or in any storage or retrieval systems without the permission in writing from the author.

ISBN 978-0-9558679-0-3

Printed and bound by CPI Antony Rowe, Eastbourne

PASSING CLOUDS

Jonathan Bennett

"The greatest friend
Of poesy, that it should be a friend
To sooth the cares, and lift the thoughts of man"

John Keats

Acknowledgements

It has often been said that writing is a solitary occupation. There is some truth in this, but only up to a point. I count myself fortunate to have rubbed shoulders with numerous scribblers over the years and I salute them all for the help they have given me by way of friendly comment and criticism. I recall in particular the valuable contact I have had with fellow members of Fleet (Hampshire) U3A Creative Writing Group, the Farnham & District (Surrey) Writers Circle and, most recently, the Petersfield (Hampshire) Writers Circle.

Let me pay tribute to my dear companion and fellow writer, Hetty Staples, for her persistent badgering to get my stuff into some kind of book form and for her subsequent help with getting my act together. I am also sincerely grateful to John Owen Smith for his expertise in setting up the mass of material that had lain in the darkness of my computer, and steering it into the light of day.

This publication is dedicated to my late, beloved wife, Stella, whose talent as an artist illumined my pathway with her ideas and her inspiration. It is with her in mind, along with many others who fought the same battle, that I have arranged for the net proceeds from sales of this book to be donated to Macmillan Cancer Support.

Jonathan Bennett

Contents

Noah's Return 7
Lullaby 8
Crocodile 10
Passing Clouds 12
Weather Warning 14
Arena 16
Stay Tuned 18
Tearaway 19
The Red Room 20
Dear Mr President 21
Harvest Festival 22
Breakout 24
If Only 26
Situation Vacant 28
Fix 30
Windows 32
Jeremy 33
Quarry 34
Spent Matches 36
Verdict 37
Equinox 38
Picnic 40
Peace Keeper 41
Crusade 42
Tournament 44
The Young Dragons 46
Vivat Vivat! 48
Lost in Translation 50

Tapestries	51
Big Wheel	52
I, Vesuvio	54
Yosemite	55
Age Concern	56
Stop Watch	58
Reflections	60
Summer Rain	61
Amelia	62
Saplings	64
Locked Doors	65
Shell Beach	66
Starbird	67
Exhibit	68
Brolly	69
Gorilla	70
Elevenses	71
First Love	72
Vacant Possession	74
Matriarch	76
Slow Drop	77
Give and Take	77

NOAH'S RETURN

The village high street
sounded once to walking feet
and passing cars.

Now a sea of dried-out mud
crazed into mosaic
by four months of drought.

Reservoir of memories.

Stone cottages on either side
observe through blue-skied sockets
old home-steaders
on their pilgrimage.

The one-time vicar
standing by the roofless church
sees tapering towards God
the steeple, now a broken tooth.

From man-made covenants
entered into years ago
the flood was organised
requiring him to lead his flock
to low-hope high-ground bungalows
five miles up the valley.

This, he thinks, is how
Old Noah might have felt
if his celestial Water Board
had let him back towards life's end
to see his launching ramp.

LULLABY

For her
it was as though a sad bewitching choir
hummed high-pitched threads of sound
bringing her maimed joy
and laying claim to her.

For him
it was entirely clear.
Just another common thief.
Well dressed this one
not your usual crumpled little mouse.

The song within her
sobbed and broke
and might perhaps have stopped
but for her fear of what would then be heard
and could not be endured.

He took note of the tiny baby shoes
two pairs of small white socks
a little cotton gown
the pale blue plastic rattle -
harmless infant bric-a-brac.

Out in the street
his shadow fell across the pram,
empty but for stolen grains
of stricken hopes
made briefly warm by melodies.

Issued the usual warning -
polite regret according to the book.
A few words please
back in the store
A matter of twelve pounds forty-three.

The pale eyes reached towards the man
signalling the song within
which in that instant
touched and stained him
as might a bead of blood.

Watched her wheel her pram away
and made no move.
Thought he heard fleetingly
a mewing strain of cradle melody
borne thinly on the traffic-laden air.

CROCODILE

From this far vantage point
and with this powerful sensory device,
we have learned much
about that strange and troubled planet
which is, dear colleagues, very like our own.

It teems with life.
Its cities swarm with riotous intelligence
and yet it cloaks our data banks with fog.
The adult minds that clog that distant world
cannot be read or penetrated.

Only the uncluttered thoughts of children,
unspoiled as yet by avarice or guilt,
escape and wing across the great galactic curve
to touch our screens at last,
translated into myriad points of light.

Our computers have been shepherding
this torch-lit innocence into one long line,
forming on your screens a bright procession -
allowing us to learn from all that youth
before its fragile wisdom over-grows and dies.

Watch first of all the adolescent group
leading the carnival and tainted heavily by now
with threshold adult thoughts.
See how the light of childhood is already blurred
as though by drifting smoke across the printed page.

Those next in line are younger
and hence the flame burns brighter.
Yet here and there we can perceive
a gaseous blue-ish tint of fear
hinting at horrors beyond our comprehension.

Observe the minds of babies, small and white.
They burn like altar candles
that flicker randomly, as though some gentle breath
has stirred within them tiny virgin dreams,
tranquil as the early light of dawn.

Last and most wondrous of all, dear friends,
look at the tail, a carnival of needle-lights
stretching and winding to infinity.
The meaning of this awesome sight eludes us -
we simply do not know.

It is our prayerful urgent dream,
miraculous if true,
that this is their plantation of seed-life,
a trillion million child-souls in the womb
waiting to be born.

PASSING CLOUDS

Near journey's end
the lively west wind
dragged its frayed white lace
across the wave-tops
and flung ragged faces
laughing through the sky.

In the bar that first day out
we'd met and talked
each within ourselves
and yet, though locked
in shipboard sanctuaries
minds touched briefly
feather-edged like clouds.

That final day
sea-spray on my cheek
a racing cloud took on her face
and from that wild tumultuous sky
smiled down a soft farewell.

Never a shipboard passion this.
No furtive couplings
in either single cabin.
Just talk and no talk
warming hands
before the same small sun.

Went down below
to look for her
and say goodbye
but never found her.

Back on deck
a half-hour on
the slackened wind
cradled half-remembered dreams
like dockside flotsam
half-adrift and half-ashore.

Uniformly blue the sky
though flecked with memories

empty of clouds.

WEATHER WARNING

It has returned again
as plain as day
once more to taunt
as it has always done
on land and sea
since birth.

This time it has become
a yellow marker buoy
just off my starboard bow
riding easily
the angry white-topped waves.

So time to fight again,
to haul on jib and mainsheet
hardening sail
heeling dangerously the slender craft,
making me
lean body-weight to windward
skimming the abrasive sea.

Five roaring minutes
drag out like an hour of war,
sparring with a Force Seven blow,
cleaving through a hostile tide
in full Spring flood.

When all is done
the buoy is there again
away to starboard
dancing its frenetic jig
on compass bearing as before,
showing that my speed
has been precisely
zero knots.

At another time and place
the weather mark may loom again
in some new guise, who knows?

Maybe as a yellow lantern
swinging in the dark
to mock and tease
all those whose instinct is
to beat against the tide
and tack upwind
alone.

ARENA

The stadium tunnel
amplifies his breath
to roaring pain
in tearing lungs.

Some separate alien heart
beats in his head, impelling
motion to unfeeling feet.
Nothing of his doing -

nothing any more
but a balloon of light
enlarging now to burst
into a gong of spacious sound.

Ten thousand voices
merge as one
though he must tell himself
it is the adversary's roar
before the final lethal pounce.

Stumbles like a poisoned ant
elbows scrubbing gravel,
lion-breath on his neck
rancid in his nostrils.

Choirs of energy lift him up -
rekindling some small flame
forcing hope and movement
willing him, until

head raised to sky
teeth bared
arms spread like wings
chest thrusting
to the sinking of the blade
into the throat, he feels at last
the butterfly caress
of winning tape.

Now a different kinder roar.
Warm waterfall applause
of victory.

Tender hands bring peace.
He smiles.
Gold-medal gladiator
has slain the secret lion
in his head.
It was his doing after all.

STAY TUNED

We'll be back with further news
after the break.

The first half-minute
is devoted to the virtues
of the latest model from Japan.
Lush upholstery, with just a hint
of stylishly performed rear-seat adultery

Observe the latest mobile.
It does everything except sit up and beg,
and therefore surely merits
prime-time exhortation.

Throw in a little after-shave, and finally
delicious cholesterol temptation
offered by the new quadruple burger
with crinkly-cut French fries.

Welcome back to News at Ten Part 2
in which we bring
reports of new atrocities in Baghdad
famine in Soudan
the murder of two Britons in Miami
and the late football results.

TEARAWAY

Appeared at first on satellite,
a cloudy rosette in the Gulf of Mexico.

Weather stations on alert
could only then observe
as playful Charlie scooped the sea
and tipped it over Florida,
dismantling with infant glee
parts of the causeway to Key West.

Charlie crossed the State-line into Georgia,
a self-sufficient child who broke no laws
since none applied to him, but who
with uproar and impunity
ploughed a swathe of chaos.

Died, weak and whimpering
in southern Carolina

Sibling Daniel followed up behind.
cyclonic-mad with rage
in search of hostages
with which to finish
what his brother had begun.

THE RED ROOM

Joy and grief
blackmail and bribe
adoration and goodbyes
all neatly sealed in envelopes
for privacy.

See how they are nudged
without much thought
through that dark doorless entrance.
Entry to the red room after all is simple
The only problem is there's no retreat.

My letter to you hovers
trembling at finger-tips
like some sweet life about to be released.
The urge is not to let it go
for fear of such finality.

And so at last I do it with a sigh.
Discover a momentary self
weightless, slightly drunk
ecstatic and at peace.

It's up to the Collector now.

DEAR MR PRESIDENT

We understand completely
Mr President
and are sure that we can help.
Your need to maintain order
using modern and efficient means
is well appreciated.

The weapons we supply come all complete
with ample stocks of ammunition.
Training manuals are provided.
Targets are a matter
for your individual choice.

Long-term credit is available
on most attractive terms, whereby
you only start to pay
when you have won the day.

When that day comes
call us again
and we will gladly pledge
humanitarian aid -
tents and blankets for the dispossessed
food for the starving
drugs and medicines for the sick.

It is our policy to assist
Third World development
by means of trade and aid,
with satisfaction guaranteed
dear Mr President
to all those
whom it may concern.

HARVEST FESTIVAL

Beneath the feel-good canopy
smooth team work from the congregation
colours truth with fiction.

> *We thank you, Lord*
> *for these Your bounteous gifts*
> *and pray that those who give*
> *be blessed no less than those*
> *who shall receive.*

Outside
unceremonious rainfall scythes the night
with splinters of expiring hope.

Late-comer, with her offering
bundled at her breast,
face porcelain-white, eyes wet
with more than rain,
finds the great oak door clamped tight
against unfestive interruption
of established order and thanksgiving.

Places the small bundle on the step.
Thin fingers wrap the shawl
more closely round the tiny face
all sleepy-pink and unaware.

In gesture to the opaque night
she stands and raises matchstick arms
signalling, as it would seem,
the sounding of a single organ note,
soft, mellow and sustained
to those within.

The people, all unknowing, rise
moved by the sound to ritual prayer
to be forgiven for forgotten sin.

> *Lord have mercy on us.*
> *Christ have mercy on us.*
> *Lord have mercy on us.*

Silent figure, willow-thin
now hugging nothing to herself but loss
hears through the stone
a momentary strain of hymn-tune
fading and merging with her
into the unillumined night.

BREAKOUT

For fifteen minutes, twice a month
through all that empty web of years
our only act of love
was spun with anguished finger-tips
through armour-plated glass.

The prison bars have gone now
but their shadows are still real enough,
striping freedom with new, dull detention.

Nothing has changed.
The web continues its grey calendar.
Her questing fingers on my flesh
still press on glass, chill and invisible.
Only our eyes meet and embrace
in small and frightened coitus.

Along her pale moon-naked breast
where there should be sweet shelter in warm dunes
my fingers, as if thimbled in numb steel
encounter marbled cold.

Only the tears on her sad face are warm.
These I can feel, salt to the taste
as are my own.

There, surely, is the breakout route –
mapping our way
down tributary rivulets of shared tears
into wider, kinder waters.
It has to be a path ordained
by instruments of trust
navigating by the stars inside our heads
beneath a secret sky uncut by searchlight beams
downstream to the sea.

Not soon.
It will take time to rid ourselves
of razor-wire and watch towers
but if we take care never to look back
and simply stay together
armoured glass could melt at last,
bringing sweet release.

Sentence then would end.

IF ONLY

Here goes then, children,
With some typical examples.

Time was
when ecstasy was legal
and not in capsule form.

Bent coppers only came about
from pennies balanced on the track
and being gay was simply
to be happy as a pig.

In times more innocent than now
carpets got laid, not people
and damaged clothing got stitched up
instead of court-room juries.

No longer cast upon the waters
bread today is what you earn or steal
so you can buy a loaf.

A watershed was where the river
first saw light
in some quiet upland slope.
Never was it until now a barrier
to youthful TV viewers late at night.

Point taken, children? Fine,
for you can bet your turn will come
in twenty-five years time (or thereabouts)
when you might tell your offspring
much the same as I now say to you

If only
words already measured
could be husbanded as diamonds,
deep-shrined in some space-time continuum
impervious to the cold steel chisels
of tomorrow's lexicographers.

SITUATION VACANT

Take a seat, dear chap, he beams.
Voice as dark brown as his suit.
Reassuring, man-to-man, to intimate
we're both men of intelligence.

> *And so begins encounter no. 34*
> *resulting from my letter no. 156*
> *sweated from long nightmares in the dark.*

Two minutes to discuss the weather
cordially, as per the book
to put a dear chap at his ease.
Smiles and sighs
to show his worry is as keen as mine.

Your excellent CV, he says
is nothing less than a citation of achievement.
How can I be sure that such a man
could rest content
in such a quiet tributary as this?

> *How indeed?*
> *Nor can he know the silent mockery*
> *that accompanies the hand-out*
> *of the Job Seekers Allowance every week.*

A most distinguished record,
really quite commendable, he states.
Eye-to-eye in level contact
simulating strict equality.

> *Anxious soft eyes reaching*
> *to greet me in the hallway,*
> *seeing with no need of instant words*
> *my further diminution.*

Voice painted now in ebony
to cloak the falling blow.
The truth, dear friend, is this.

> *Never mind, dear love, she breathes*
> *her lips soft on my cheek*
> *You've got another interview next week.*

Shakes my hand with finely-tuned sincerity.
I won't insult you with this job, he says,
because you don't need me to tell you
you' re vastly over-qualified.

FIX

In memory of Stephanie

Time for my next trip
up Treason Mountain.

I used to know the reason why
it got this name from me
but now I have forgotten.

Perhaps it was that then I thought
the view from that high pinnacle
would be of Paradise
not normally available
this side of death.

And so I fed my blood with viscous smoke
that winged my feet
and sang me upward to a crest
where for a while
I breathed imagined oxygen
and fashioned hollow beauteous dreams
wherein to bury old realities.

The slow descent down that far slope
was gentle-tempered
smooth and effortless.
Only gradually and late
did I become aware of shadows
cast by crags of Treason Mountain Two.

Its peak was loftier than the first
and therefore more desirable.
I readied up my soul again
with one last supper
for just one more reconnaissance.

There have been many suppers since
and each has cost me silver from my soul.
Paradise is out there somewhere.

I have bags of silver left.

OK, OK
don't worry so.
I can handle it.
You'll see

WINDOWS

For just this one week of the year
we have placed windows
on these faceless walls.

This is our transaction.

Come through the turnstile
and observe a hundred universes
gathered in framed openings
that lead from your world into ours
and from us to you.

We are there too.

The poetry of light and shade
and captive scents of pastel hues
give us good vantage
from which to view you in return.

Let us depict you to yourself.

Indifference possibly
or even boredom (all too often)
but just occasionally
pain or pleasure shining in your eyes
reflecting joy or grief
from some distressful beauty
discovered in our world
or remembered from your own.

Reward enough for us
that after windows close
and we have gone
some warm breath might remain
to mist your memory with faint dreams
fashioned by crayon point or sable tip
into fragile immortality.

JEREMY

In memory of the late Jeremy Batten, who was Chairman of Farnham & District Writers Circle at the time of his death in 1997.

He came out of the morning sun,
a gentle, minstrel prince.
He sat and yarned with us a while,
dispensing golden gifts
of mirth and wit.

Then came eclipse
bringing twilight
and untimely night –
an unsought ending
to the early afternoon.

Look up into the cloudless night
and you may see a camp-fire
made from stars
round which the minstrel sits
with new companionship.

Be still
and listen.
Listen carefully
and you may hear
the laughter of the gods.

QUARRY

Foam-flecked with terror,
flat-eared, tail dead straight
aerodynamic as an arrow-head
he fled.

Blood lyrics from the hounds
orchestrated death
with scarlet pageantry
and a clarion horn.

Patterns splintered
as a leading horseman crashed,
felled by a slender tethered wire
that flecked the carnival with sabotage.

Darting through dereliction
the saboteur's sharp eye alighted
on a glint of gold.
Seized it hungrily and ran.

That night he walked the city street
and swung the pocket watch with joy,
grinned as street-lights scattered stars
along the dangling rose-gold chain.

A shadow separated from the nearby dark
Harsh glint of steel flashed briefly,
eclipsing gold and burying yesterday's success
where tomorrow would forget.

One hundred alien miles away
a huntsman nursed a fractured collar-bone
and cursed whoever had made off
with his beloved heirloom watch.

Quite close at hand
a dog fox rested, chin on paws,
yesterday forgotten
tomorrow inconceivable.

Nostrils twitched
with aromatic present certainties
and the sweet serenity
of now.

SPENT MATCHES

He shivered in the London park.
Watched the small clouds scud
across the sky
like tiny doubts that wanted to efface
old certainties.

Filled his pipe with favourite ready-rubbed
and opened up the match box
to reveal, as always,
shrivelled burned-out skeletons
in memory of his youth.

Christian Mission in North Borneo.
Village mud-deep in the rain-soaked forest.
Trying to light his pipe.
Match after damp match failing to ignite.
The box a tiny grave of still-born births.

Fifty long years on
he maintained requiem for those small lost lives
by revering all those others that had lived
to give their destined brief performance
followed by unceremonious death.

He found among the charred remains
a single good match waiting to fulfil itself
but which he could not bring himself to strike.
Might not this be his life,
and the only one, the last?

The clouds grew heavier within,
imprinting mid-faith crisis
on the skyscape of his mind.
Pipe unlit, he pocketed the box
wherein reposed that sweet last chance.

Shrinking from the deepening chill
he turned his unquiet mind once more
to firming up his sermon
for next Evensong –
on Everlasting Life.

VERDICT

A wizened four feet two she was
and easily past eighty I would guess.
"Good morning, Mrs Green," I said.
"I'm the man from Neighbourcare
to pick you up and take you
to your weekly physio."

My old umbrella fought with wind and rain.
She pointed with her white cane at the sky
and smilingly said "I can see the sun,"
denoting vision of a kind I could not share.

I put her thin wrist on my sleeve
and helped her to the car.

"Why d'you do this job then, dear?" she asked.
"You must have better things to do."
I laughed. "Retirement occupation," I replied.
"It stops me having too much time to think."

Of course, the usual barriers were in place.
Couldn't tell her of old scores I had
to settle with myself from years ago.
Saw again the family I had once betrayed.
Remembered all those shady deals I'd done
that left the punters wrecked.
New Brownie points were needed nowadays
to cancel out old treacheries.

Had to help her in the car.
Lifted into place her swollen leg.
She scrutinised me closely with her sightless eyes.
"Give it time, dear Mr Neighbourcare" she said.
"You'll be OK."

I handed in her thin white stick
Thought to myself, it's I that have the need for that
not her
and started up the car.

EQUINOX

Small brothers played their introspective games.
One built a grand line of defensive fortresses.
The other drew a straight line in the sand
bisecting two great ramparts of the enemy.

Blows were exchanged.
Blood brotherhood was shed
eliciting a cloy of hatred, born of seeds
long germinated from some ancient past.

Their father came to act as referee.
"We'll all return tomorrow," he declared
"Meanwhile we'll let old Father Neptune judge."
As he spoke, the tide began to turn.

Next morning, with the sun low on the sea,
the brothers looked down from a vantage point
to see the beach as seamless and devoid of art
as it had looked when all the earth was young.

They gazed in sullen hate and disbelief.
Each saw himself as deviously tricked
by Neptune who could never understand
that this result was unacceptable.

Manhood brought riches and success to both.
One bought a merchant bank to house his spite.
The other spent his wealth on legal cannonry.
Neither one prevailed. Both died in poverty.

The golden citadel was razed to pay off debts
and all the weaponry was traded off for scrap
leaving only headstones in a cliff-top cemetery
closely side by side with no boundary between.

Below the cliff-top, on a silken beach
two tiny grandsons practised individual arts.
One tipped out watch-towers from his upturned pail
The other scratched out patterns in the sand.

In some far distant deep, a memory stirred.
Swift currents bore old signals to the ocean's edge.
Sleepy wavelets at low-water mark awoke
gained strength and bared their small white teeth.

The tide was on the turn again.

PICNIC

He stared wide-eyed
as sweet New Mother broke the crisp baguette,
scattering seeds of sesame
across the clean white cloth.

Beyond his stare he saw Old Mother
starved and stately, upright, insect-thin
gazing at the sky.

The child, thus prompted, raised his eyes
towards a cloud-flecked canopy of porcelain blue.
Saw instead a bronze medallion sun
set in a carapace of cruel blue steel.

Looked down again towards the picnic cloth
spread white on meadow-green.
Saw New Mother's honeyed hand
setting plates and cups
among the seeds of sesame.

Observed his own small hand
deep ebony with ragged finger nails
scratching carefully for seeds
between the withered plants.

New Mother watched with wonder
as the child picked up the seeds
missing not a single one
and passed them to her
mixed with whispered words

Please
You must eat all of these
so you shall not die today

PEACE KEEPER

White with tension, eyes alert
the soldier bade his cursory goodbyes.
Time to set out on patrol again
through territory spiked with death.

Oblivious to the menace underfoot
peaceful shoppers sleep-walked.
Commuters rushed, corn-flaked and comatose
and children danced between trip wires
that lay like lizards in their path.

He spied them all, the wires of death.
With panther stealth, he placed each foot
square in the centre of each concrete flag
along the pavement on the way to school.

Total concentration brought him tragedy.
Collision with the school-gate copper
flung him from a sniper's bullet to his knees
and sent him sprawling over two trip wires.

Oh shit, he cried, *I'm dead !*

Dreaming again, young Jim? the copper asked.
You'll get it in the neck for being late.

The boy looked at the blood-stain on his hand.
He saw instead the carnage of mankind.
He saw guilt trickle down his thumb.
He saw his mission as peace keeper end.

It doesn't matter any more the boy replied.
The world has just blown up.

CRUSADE

If you are naughty just once more
(my father used to say)
the dragon in the stairwell cave
will swallow you for lunch.

Some decades on
I took a trip, long promised to myself
to slay the big green monster
in the house where I was born.

But I was cheated of revenge.
The house was gone and in its place
now ranged a supermarket, glittering and brash
wherein no monsters were allowed to play.

Inside I wandered to the spot where once
the entrance to the stairwell must have been
but now the way lay blocked by shelves
of Corn Flakes, Weetabix and Shredded Wheat.

Can I help you, dear? the lady asked.
I'm looking for the dragon, I replied.
She smiled at me without surprise
and handed me a Corn Flake pack.

Back in the car
I opened up the box
lifted out the bag of flakes, and there below
reposed my lifelong enemy.

Stripped of lies
and adult alibis
my dragon sat, inert in plastic, mossy-green
and all of seven centimetres long.

He looked at me
with smiling wicked eyes
and whispered through the old dreams
that were tattooed in my brain.

This is all I am, he said
and all I ever was.
The rest was acquiescent fear
which now you have undone.

I drove off, night-mare free,
yet knowing what a small and fragile thing
my childhood used to be.
and still is to this day.

TOURNAMENT

Two minutes of the second half to go.

He watched, numb with despair
while troops ignored his mother's screams
and led her man away.

From centre-field
the ball passed skating to his feet.
Trapped it firmly, then
dribbled it at speed just inside touch.

The crowd roared
drowning out the snarl
of grinding caterpillar tracks.
The tank began its sullen task
with slow deliberation
to flatten all that he had known
from the day that he was born.

Through the rubble
fifty metres distant
sunlight framed in white posts, waiting.
A reason for his life.

Brushed aside the enemy and shot.
The ball curved
graceful as a hawk
silencing the din of war.
Homed to its nest
in the corner of the net.

The terraces exploded
in writhing patterned ballet
of the nation's colours, red and black
Sank to his knees, tears flowing
wordless for the father
he would never see again.

The final whistle sounded
and he raised his arms
fists clenched in tight salute.
Thanksgiving whispered in his head
that for this victory
no-one would be led away to die.

THE YOUNG DRAGONS

The young child-parent hovers
at the ocean's edge.
Two threads curve out from him
one towards land, the other out to sea
the first invisible
the other nearly so.

He laughs with anxious joy to see
the bright dance of the dragon-child
tethered by an arc of twine
and struggling to be free.

The parent-woman watches
from the shadow of the old sea-wall
her sleek young son
eyes solicitous with love for him.

The day will come
when I must let him go
for he will no more need
this cob-web life-line that extends
from my strong hand to his
but not just yet, please God,
not yet.

She summons him to reel his dragon in
startling the child
dead-locking him in stasis
and loosening his frail hand-hold
on the slender thread.

He wails despair
and almost runs into the waves
to curb the paper-dragon's flight.
Observes it wheel and loop
in doomed ecstatic consort
with cousin-clouds migrating
windborne towards the lowering sun.

The second bond holds firm
strung somewhere psyche-deep
where land and water meet.
The woman clasps her son to her,
dries his tears and promises him
another kite next day.

The line has held this time.
Let it be so for just this little while.
That day will surely come
but not quite yet, please God,
not yet.

VIVAT VIVAT!

They raised him
from that fierce first death;
a Lazarus in stone
set on a marble platform
to last a thousand years.

The rebirth was unveiled
to iron fanfares for old cruelties.
The Royal Guard presented arms
to honour tyranny
while cannons at the river's edge
belched in salute
to quench the whipcrack echoes
of half a million deaths.

A well-rehearsed, conscripted girl
laid at the mighty plinth
a wreath of daffodils.

The ceremony done
the regal escort clattered back to base
and crowds of sullen watchers melted
into shadows as the curfew fell.

Alone the despot stood
with right arm raised
as though to conjure homage
from a million grateful serfs.
The face, soft with compassion
from floodlights cunningly deployed,
broadcast benevolence and wisdom
to be engraved on tablets
of contorted history.

A score of aching winters wrought contempt.
Chiselled handsomeness gave way
to scabrous injury from acid rain.
The leonine head became
a guanoed perch for clowning gulls,
while furtive citizens spat quietly
on pocked graffiti-sandalled feet.

The tyrant's second death was marked
by strident brutish joy.
Ragged revolutionaries
clawed the despot down
with chains about his neck.
The severed head, in final spasm, rolled
and came at last to rest
beside a nearby bed
of flowering daffodils.

LOST IN TRANSLATION

After so long
the world is sharper,
razor-edged with decibels,
strident with colour.
Harder for sure
than it ever was in there.

It's taken me a while
to meet old friends again
for language doesn't seem to work
the way it should.

The words are understandable
but the tongue says one thing
while the eyes say something else.

The hand-shake feels sincere and firm
but in the face nerves stir
and send pale messages
not easy to translate.

Today I walked among red roses
stroked their petals
soft as a woman's face
and no nerve moved in them.

Talked to the stranger
who had grown them in his garden
and the language in his eyes
was identical to theirs.

It seems then I shall have to move
to where new people and their roses live
and then things will get better.

I can't be bothered
taking language lessons
merely to interpret
what life-long friends
and erstwhile lovers
think of me today.

TAPESTRIES

Prior to that beginning
silence was the king who
longed for witnesses.
Forged carbon molecules
and gave them soundless visions,
voiceless melodies.

For just a while
particles of lattice music
threaded tapestries of life,
lavishing evidence
and confirmation
that silence was no longer king.

For just that glistening interval
the king lay maddened
powerless and dethroned
until the final echo was dispelled
and royal stillness once again
held primacy.

BIG WHEEL

Paid thirty pence
and climbed aboard the wheel.
Started gently upward
or perhaps it was
that she sank sadly downward
taking with her everything we'd dreamed.

That final quarrel minutes earlier
had honed pride to a razor's edge
necessitating flight from further damage
to myself and her.

Curved up and outward
into rediscovered adolescence
every yard an individual year
of reconstructed growth.

From way up high I could look down
at rooftops, grey with secrets,
cataracts concealing love and loss.
Somewhere among them were my own.

The ageing slow descent brought back
familiar sights and sounds
of childhood reawakened
and a longing for the zenith
only recognised when it has passed.

Wanting to re-create what used to be
I asked the man to wind the wheel back
that she might here me say
Forgive.
It was all me.
Let's try again.

Course it won't wind back, he scoffed.
This here's a Ferris Wheel
not a bleedin' railway train
and anyway you're back where you began.

I looked at emptiness where she had stood.
Not quite, I said, *but then I guess that's life.*

Too bloody right it is, he said.
You bought your ticket, made your choice.
You've had your ride, full circle
one way only.

That's your lot.

I, VESUVIO

They still insist in nesting at my feet
these fireflies.
Unworshipping and unaware
they eke out candled lives
with celebration of ignoble fantasies.

At Pompeii
I gave them rebirth of creation
that they could start to comprehend
the might of elemental purity.
Instead they kindled pale new torches
to illuminate old dreams.

They did not learn at Herculaneum
even though I quenched their glow-worm spark
and boiled the close-adjoining sea.
Still they failed to understand.

I shall sleep for yet a little while
and then, when it is time,
be warned, you nestlings of small Napoli
I shall take back what is mine.

I, Vesuvio, can wait.

YOSEMITE

They came on wild erratic trajectories –
these demons of destruction.
Converged and met in mutual prayer
inside Cathedral Rock

After thanksgiving
followed sport and recreation.
El Capitano clawed down laden clouds
and wrung out floods.

Another kicked a boulder with his boot
and set in train a thunderous avalanche.
A brother breathed a playful flame
and torched the lush green valley into ash.

Well pleased, each went his way
one back to San Andreas Fault
to further studies for a new debacle.
Others returned to white-hot anvils
in Etna and Vesuvius.

Timidly at first
slow life returned.
New nests, fresh burrows
trembled with old frissons of rebirth.

And men returned
in churning four-by-fours
and marvelled that the gods
were able to create with ease
such graceful and sublime tranquillity.

AGE CONCERN

It all began that day I lied
to gain unlawful entry to the cinema.
"It's X-certificate," she said
"How old are you?"

"Eighteen" I answered, turning slightly pink.
"Oh no you're not," the ticket-lady said,
"I know your mum quite well and you're fifteen.
I'll set my spies to keep an eye on you."

I tried to join the army after that.
"Are you eighteen?" the colour-sergeant asked.
Once more I lied, again to no effect –
the secret spies had pipped me to the post.

Years passed.
I never lied about my age again
but then I never told how old I really was
to anyone.

And yet they had to let me know they knew.
At fifty, an insurance company wrote
to indicate that at my time of life
private health care was the only thing for me.

At fifty-five, the Saga flow began
regaling me with heady old-age joys.
They sent me brochures showing youthful elderlies
abseiling in the sun.

When I reached sixty, several City banks
(of whom I'd never previously heard)
offered me "mature investor" schemes
to give me reassuring income in my twilight years.

Desperate to escape, I fled to Canada.
It took them five full years to track me down.
One of the demon-spies based in Toronto
got in touch with me.

"At sixty-five," he wrote, "You can have peace of mind.
A mere fifty dollars once a month
will guarantee in full your funeral costs
and lift this burden from your grieving family."

I know that when I'm knocking on that Final Door
there'll be a notice on it that will say
"Welcome, friend, we've been expecting you today."
And on it in large print will be my name

with time and date of birth.

STOP WATCH

On New Year's Eve
precisely at 11.59
time stopped.

The little silver heart
that had for so long pulsed
now quietly stilled the second hand
one minute from that magic hour.

I mourned the dead watch on my wrist,
a precious love-gift that was part of me.
Never took it off – slept and swam in it.
New Year would have to wait.

Had trouble finding a replacement heart.
No jeweller had a transplant match
so New Year was postponed
and put on hold.

By April 10 I'd found a heart to fit.
A tiny silver button from Japan.
Sat in the garden while a squirrel watched
as I gave heart to both my watch and me.

Sat tense as once again the second hand
strode strong with purpose to the midnight hour.
And when at last it crossed that magic line
I punched the air with joy.

Happy New Year, everyone, I yelled
startling the squirrel into scurrying flight
and scattering two large magpies from my lawn.
Only a blackbird on my roof remained unmoved.

It seemed to me his song was meant for me.
Its mocking lyric seemed to say
*Right year – wrong month – so I regret
to say you're not out of your wood yet.*

I looked down at my watch in deep despair.
The date read January 1 not April 10.
To put that right, I'd have to stop my watch
and wait for eight long months and twenty days.

Never mind – one hurdle over with and done.
Meanwhile I'll settle for the midnight springtime sun.

REFLECTIONS

In memory of Stephanie

That garden is still filled with flowers
more than ever I remember.
Their petals are old inner thoughts
glistening with the tears
that once were shed.

So strong the blossoms still appear
Nurtured by a sad and special kind of rain
Droplets of soul-grief.
The petals bleed
giving off reflections from within.

I walk these days
through this rain-garden
on that same path where once
I only stood just at its edge
and watched.

Used to see you
clear and golden
in the young sunlight.
Used to so rejoice in you
though you were out of reach.

Today this tear-drenched garden
continues to be only you.
I walk it freely now
treading soft soil
and wondering

wondering where you are.

SUMMER RAIN

True, the sun is higher in the sky
than once it was
heralding what used to be called
Summer.

The trouble is
that newness has been lost somewhere
in one long sullen season
with neither end nor boundary.

>My songbird daughter
>lissome creature of the wild
>raises honeyed arms above her head
>and cries with joy
>*Everything is cool*
>*The rains are coming*

Yet surely this can only be more blood
to feed the desert drought
and leave its ineradicable brand
of memories upon the skin.

>My sweeting daughter
>races down the beach
>trapping shining medals from the sky.
>She sings
>*Oh brill oh wow, at last*
>*it's raining*

And yet there is here something different
something at once both old and new
an aromatic truth
that springs from dry dust laid to rest.

These droplets cleanse
and leave no stain.
Maybe the summer rain
is really coming back again.

AMELIA

Essentially a creature of the wild,
she should be in some jungle, stalking prey
not here in England tearing up our home.
My theory is that our cat hates all men
and yet my wife insists
that all that brawling caterwauling din
which greets me when I get back home from work
is just Amelia's Siamese way of saying
that she loves me.

She has a funny way of showing it.
Take yesterday, long day, I got home hungry
ready for my favourite salmon salad –
to find it off the plate and in the cat !
She'd kindly left the lettuce and tomato
and had by now just reached the stage
of rounding off her meal
nose deep inside the jug of full-cream milk
mopping up the last exquisite drop.

I went berserk.
You noisome and disgusting bag, I screamed
and hurled my briefcase at her startled head.
It missed and crashed.
The beast escaped – the milk jug died instead.
In hot pursuit I hounded her with hate
and when I thought I really had her trapped
behind the television set
she howled and fled upstairs.

I ran in through the master bedroom door
and there she was
seated royally on the double bed.
She got up as I entered, looked me in the eye,
and peed deliberately on the counterpane.
Of course I didn't catch her, knew I never could
but one thing she and I knew well
was that I'd track her down eventually
inside her favourite lair.

Long after dark I crept upstairs
and peered behind the airing cupboard door,
Sure enough, in that snug space above the tank
on the blanket which was hers alone
Amelia slept, tail curled around her nose.
I stroked her ear.
She opened half an eye and half began to purr.
Silently I closed the door all but an inch
and stole away to bed.

SAPLINGS

Smuggled in from some soft glade
beside the far-off English Thames,
hope was that it might turn into a dream
of new fertility within this sterile dust.

Newly arrived, I could not know
that this small potted willow shoot
had no way to survive
in soil made poisonous by mania
and too much boiling blood.

Scooped a home for it in dusty shade
beside the torso of a burned-out tank
and gave the task of watering it
to little five-year old Ndola,
thinking he might gain a sibling –
stick-limbed, frail and parentless
like himself.

Loved to watch the two of them
each nurturing the other
bonded by companionship,
orphan saplings both.

Let each of them be spared the truth
that only armoured hatred
puts down lasting roots
deep in this cancerous dirt

Let them rather dream a while
of fronded groves
miraculously born of love
beneath an innocent forgiving sky.

LOCKED DOORS

Somewhat more often nowadays
as the years ahead grow less
temptation rises
beckoning from attic dust
to open that old door
long closed and barred
against a noisome past.

God knows
the key was long ago thrown out
and willingly forgotten
in favour of well-lit unlocked rooms
reflecting gentle hues of respite
that is almost peace.

Problem is
nostalgia seeps beneath the door
and creeps across the floor
like poison gas
intent on blemishing the mind
with faded symbols of old envy
in place of current happiness.

What would one find behind that door today
but fallen trees and rooms grown small?
Tall friends and dangerous foes alike
all shrunken uniformly by time's passage
drifting rudderless and irrelevant
upon a dull indifferent sea.

Better then to leave that old door locked
with old feuds buried in the attic dust
and navigate what's left
with just a simple map
made up from brilliant stars
within one's head.

Let's cut no keys to yesterday.

SHELL BEACH

Underfoot today lie villas
hovels, broken fortresses
pitted by abrasive time and tide
their histories unchronicled.

Shattered suburbs sleep
half-buried in untended cemeteries
for none but beachcombers to find
in shingle and uneasy shifting sand.

One day from this parched resting place
I plucked a princely sun palace
a regal carapace of pearl and pink
mysteriously ashine.

Warmed it gently in my hand
and pressed it to my ear.
Thought I heard the rustle of a royal robe
against a curving balustrade.

Every wave that breaks along this shore
gives off pale echoes of that pulse
that used to beat within the hearts of friends
who lived in these abandoned homes.

STARBIRD

The caravan parked quietly
in the pitch alongside mine.
Swan-white and sleek
it bore the name *Starbird*

The little girl came over.
Watched me gravely as I wrote.
"Whatchoo doing?" she enquired.
"Writing poetry," I replied.

She thought a bit.
Then she said "Who for?"
I thought a bit
and then I said "For you."

She thought some more
but then her mum called out
to come straight back at once
and glared her fear of me.

Scribbled at my Starbird poem
far into the night.
Finished it and fell asleep –
woke up late next day.

Struggled from my van to sunlight
poem in my hand
to find mere flattened grass.
Starbird had taken wing.

Waited all that day until the night
Hoping for some moon-lit trail
down which my Starbird poem
could meander to her home.

Wondered to myself
which one of all those million stars
was unpoliced by fear of poetry.
Hoped she might be there.

EXHIBIT

Only the original exists
and is available for public view
but positively not for sale.

Being by definition infinite
the dimensions are problematical
and thereby render it unsuitable
for mounting or enclosure in a frame.

It simply hangs there as it always has –
a miracle of shape and space
forever changing and yet constant
executed and re-executed in mixed media
throughout all time.

We have entitled it the universe
and seek to copy it in prayerful pigment
resulting in small monuments
and limited editions of reality.

As to the creator of this masterpiece
there continues to be much dispute.
Many names have been suggested.
but it has never been resolved

It seems the artist must remain anonymous.

BROLLY

The lady picked me up and opened me.
I spread my bat-wing like a jungle bloom.
Black fabric whispered as she twirled me round.
"I'll take this one," she said and out we went
from the shop into the pouring rain.

Held hands with her and spread my mantle.
Felt the joyful first-time clatter of the shower
as waterfalls trailed shining bright
from all eight of my finger tips.
Thus began illusory fulfilment.

Saw her through four winters in the north
until a Force Ten tore me from her grasp.
Blew me inside out and carried me
into a hawthorn tree.
I needed stitches.

She didn't really want me after that.
I finished up inside the Oxfam shop
and thence via land and sea
to this far place where pouring rain
is prayed for and yet rarely seen.

My new name here is Canopy
denoting fresh utility and purpose.
My erstwhile pristine mantle is in shreds
The stitches have all burst and given way.
No longer could I cope with northern skies.

Daylight hours these days are shared
with this small half-starved girl.
She gains some respite from the mutilating sun,
while I glean from that fragile gift
my long awaited destiny.

Fulfilment.

GORILLA

Eye contact through the bars
kindles synaptic inter-action
and opens up a language-free exchange
of questions without answers.

Awesome impenetrable intelligence
tries to trace the eye-line trail
from me to him and back again,
a journey without destination.

With no disturbance
to our eye-ball comradeship
he peels a slow banana with detachment
Munches it with dull disinterest

Can he speak with plants and stars
or has he long forgotten all that jungle lore?
Can he ever know what freedom means
unless he also knows that he is caged?

He shifts his gaze at last to privacy
and thus the trail is lost.
Contact is broken by retreat
or possibly mere wave-length boredom.

Turns his back with heavy grace,
destined never to become aware
that it is we out here, not he
who live behind the bars.

ELEVENSES

Thank you. Yes
I'd love some.
How would I like it?
Ah!

The beans for preference
(culled from a mature plantation
in southern Paraguay)
are best ground with a wooden pestle
followed by six minutes in your oven
pre-heated at Mark 6 ten minutes in advance.

The water meanwhile
should be carefully prepared
from a bottle (newly-opened)
of choicest Highland Spring
brought slowly to just short of boiling-point.

Blend the mixture in a jug
of semi-porous earthenware
and let it brew awhile
in surroundings of dense-steam humidity.

Serve exquisitely
with cream of goat's milk,
seven millimetres deep,
floated from a silver spoon
to sit like snow
on some quiet mountain-top.

However
as your coffee-pot
has not survived its flight
across the room
(grazing my ear en route),
please be assured
a mug of Instant Decaf
will entirely suffice.

FIRST LOVE

In that small drab cafe
it was as though my youth had ended
with one last cup of tea
for I was eighteen
and my country needed me to be a man.

Her eyes of cobalt blue
spilled sadness on my cheek.
I tried to soften desolation with a joke.
What a way to say goodbye I sighed
with cups of tea at tuppence-ha'penny each.

Here we are in 1944, I said.
Let's have another cup in Year 2000.
By then it will have gone up to a pound.
Course it wont she uttered scornfully
You must be going daft.

The juggernaut of war changed everything.
Didn't see my first love any more
although eventually
I did run up against the Year 2000.
Knew exactly what I had to do.

Searched high and low
sought long-lost contacts from the past.
Ransacked old addresses
each leading to another in a chain
and found her at long last.

The matron showed me to the lounge
and there she was deep in a favourite chair.
Two cups of tea lay quietly between us.
Gazed deep into those eyes of cobalt blue
that offered neither tears nor recognition.

Tremulous, I gently laid my hand
on withered petal finger-tips.
I whispered *Why should you remember me?*
but from within her twilight world
came not a spark of light.

Tell you what, I ventured with a smile.
You pay a pound each for these cups of tea today.
You were ripped off then, my lad, she said.
They're only tuppence-ha'penny each.
I burst out laughing. She laughed too and said

You must be going daft.

VACANT POSSESSION

This bijou property
is currently unoccupied
and lends itself to opportunity
for an adventurous owner
to apply creative thought.

> *Stinging nettles reach with quiet belligerence*
> *to eradicate the pathway to the door.*
> *The keyhole which these many years*
> *has never echoed to a key's embrace*
> *affords sweet sanctuary*
> *to a spider and his family.*

The tranquil setting offers a retreat
from all the cares of urban life
as well as giving sanctuary
to growing children
and their much-prized pets.

> *Beneath the rotting staircase in the hall*
> *a family of adders have installed their home.*
> *No sound disturbs them*
> *save the soothing monotone*
> *of swarming bluebottles and flies*
> *inside the near-by downstairs loo.*

The southern aspect
offers matchless bedroom views
of unspoiled downland scenes
that vary richly through the seasons
giving priceless satisfaction.

> *Within the cob-webbed upstairs room*
> *two feral cats lie napping in the gloom*
> *well able later to escape by night*
> *out through the broken window-pane*
> *and down the ivy coverlet.*

This unusual property merely needs
a little tender loving care.

> *The taxi idles quietly*
> *while she just stands and watches*
> *leaning heavily on her stick.*
> *Scant white hair moves thinly in the breeze.*
> *Small white hanky flutters briefly on her cheek.*
> *At last she climbs back in and leaves*
> *to form dream-patterns in her mind*
> *of memories, of bonding*
> *and of closure.*

Any reasonable offer considered.

MATRIARCH

Armed with love
she glided from the stars.

Built her home from earth and air
Cradled us from babyhood
warmed us with her own invented fire
and quenched our thirst with
all her conjured seas.

Came zenith adulthood.
Our joyful childplay gave itself to lust
and shared delights were changed
into a dark apocalypse
of granite dreams.

We turned on Mother Nature.
Tore down her fronded ancient home.
Subjected her to wanton rape and pillage.
Threw her body back into the stars.

One day perhaps
She may be born again
in some new distant galaxy
where kind and wiser progeny
will reward her loving parenthood.

SLOW DROP

My mind is sadly
anti-gravitational.
Pennies drop slowly.

GIVE AND TAKE

Let's get first things first.
You can have the pot of gold.
I'll take the rainbow.